Self, Small, Independent Publishers' Guide and Checklist

Book Title

Author

Imprint

The Self, Small, Independent Publishers' Guide and Checklist is a product of Mythical Legends Publishing.
ISBN: 978-1-943958-61-0
Copyright © 2020 by Mythical Legends Publsihing
First Edition Published 2020
         9 8 7 6 5 4 3 2 1

Self, Small, Independent Publisher Guide and Checklist

BOOK TITLE:

☐ paperback ☐ hardback ☐ ebook ☐ audiobook

AUTHOR(s):

ILLUSTRATOR(s):

EDITOR(s):

Book Summary:

GENRE(s)

Sci-fi	Fantasy	Horror	Romance	Western	Thriller

Library Congress Control Number

SSIP Network Node

Self, Small, Independent Publisher Guide and Checklist

ISBNs:

PAPERBACK   PRICE

6 x 9		
5 x 8		
4.37 x 7		

HARDBACK   PRICE

6.14 x 9.21		
6 x 9		
5 x 8		

EBOOK   PRICE

KINDLE		
EPUB		
PDF		

AUDIOBOOK   PRICE

SSIP Network Node

Author Location List

Create Author entry in Payment System

Physical Address -

Contact Phone Number:

Email Address:

Payment:

☐ Check ☐ Wire ☐ PayPal ☐ Other

☐ Blog page:
☐ Twitter:
☐ Facebook:
☐ Instagram:
☐ Goodreads:
☐ Website:
☐ Tumblr:
☐ TikTok:
☐
☐

Self, Small, Independent Publisher Guide and Checklist

AUTHOR Checklist

- [ ] Contract
- [ ] Photo
- [ ] Bio
  - [ ] Writing Background
  - [ ] Brief History
    - [ ] When and where were you born?
    - [ ] When did you start writing?
    - [ ] Early inspirations?
    - [ ] Some life experience
    - [ ] What is your current status and location?
- [ ] Author Interview
  - [ ] Why this book?
  - [ ] When did you start writing?
  - [ ] Are there any specific authors' whose style or subject matter inspired your book?
  - [ ] Do you/did you have a support group?
  - [ ] Do you have another project in the works? If so, what is it?

SSIP Network Node

Side Notes:

Self, Small, Independent Publisher Guide and Checklist

Meeting Notes:

SSIP Network Node

Side Notes:

Self, Small, Independent Publisher Guide and Checklist

Meeting Notes:

SSIP Network Node

Side Notes:

Self, Small, Independent Publisher Guide and Checklist

Meeting Notes:

SSIP Network Node

Side Notes:

Self, Small, Independent Publisher Guide and Checklist

Meeting Notes:

SSIP Network Node

Side Notes:

Self, Small, Independent Publisher Guide and Checklist

Meeting Notes:

SSIP Network Node

Audio-Video Notes:

Self, Small, Independent Publisher Guide and Checklist

Book Marketing - PODcast and Video (Youtube, etc..)

SSIP Network Node

Sales Sheet Notes:

Self, Small, Independent Publisher Guide and Checklist

Book Marketing - Sales Sheets and Posters

SSIP Network Node

Book Reviewer Notes:

Self, Small, Independent Publisher Guide and Checklist

Book Reviewers

Name:

Email Address/DM:

Mailing Address:

Name:

Email Address/DM:

Mailing Address:

Name:

Email Address/DM:

Mailing Address:

SSIP Network Node

Book Reviewer Notes:

Self, Small, Independent Publisher Guide and Checklist

Book Reviewers

Name:

Email Address/DM:

Mailing Address:

Name:

Email Address/DM:

Mailing Address:

Name:

Email Address/DM:

Mailing Address:

SSIP Network Node

Book Reviewer Notes:

Self, Small, Independent Publisher Guide and Checklist

Book Reviewers

Name:

Email Address/DM:

Mailing Address:

Name:

Email Address/DM:

Mailing Address:

Name:

Email Address/DM:

Mailing Address:

SSIP Network Node

Book Reviewer Notes:

Self, Small, Independent Publisher Guide and Checklist

Book Reviewers

Name:

Email Address/DM:

Mailing Address:

Name:

Email Address/DM:

Mailing Address:

Name:

Email Address/DM:

Mailing Address:

SSIP Network Node

NOTES:

Self, Small, Independent Publisher Guide and Checklist

SSIP Network Node

Self, Small, Independent Publisher Guide and Checklist

SSIP Network Node

www.ingramcontent.com/pod-product-compliance
Lightning Source LLC
Chambersburg PA
CBHW070037040426
42333CB00040B/1706